The Only
FIRE

That Extinguishes

Witchcraft

[Prayers Included]

Ebenezer & Abigail
Gabriels

ISBN - 9781950579969

Ebenezer & Abigail Gabriels
19644 Club House Road Suite 815
Gaithersburg, Maryland 20886
www.EbenezerGabriels.Org
hello@ebenezergabriels.org

DEDICATION

On the altar of worship to Yahweh
Spirit of power come down
To consume the sacrifice of praise
Fire from heaven fall
fire from heaven fall

Lord we pray, let the fire from heaven fall, as it was on
Mount Carmel, and extinguish every power of witchcraft,
and God's people will be set free, in Jesus Name

CONTENT

1

~

DECODING WITCHCRAFT

Witchcraft spirit is one of the deadliest enemies of the believer. Any man or woman who is marked for God's glory will have to win the war against the spirit of witchcraft. It is not unavoidable. The only people who will avoid this war are those who have accepted defeat. Today's believers who are named by the name of Christ need to be able to decode witchcraft operations, otherwise, there will be no progress into purpose. To tackle witchcraft and uncover its activity in your life, you need to equip yourself with the knowledge of God concerning this subject. Believers already have a fire inside of them to extinguish witchcraft, however, not many believers know this. The power of witchcraft

BIBLICAL EXPLANATION OF WITCHCRAFT

David's Revelation of Witchcraft Shared With Solomon
1. Proverbs 1:14 :*for their feet rush into evil, they are swift to shed blood.*
2. Proverbs 4:16 : *for they cannot rest until they do evil; they are robbed of sleep til they make someone stumble.*

Isaiah's Revelation of Witchcraft
Beyond these descriptions; Isaiah is given the revelation of witchcraft in the 59th chapter of his book:

> *Their cobwebs are useless for clothing; they cannot cover themselves with what they make. Their deeds are evil deeds, and acts of violence are in their hands.Their feet rush into sin; they are swift to shed innocent blood. They pursue evil schemes; acts of violence mark their ways. The way of peace they do not know; there is no justice in their paths. They have turned them into crooked roads; no one who walks along them will know peace.*

Ezekiel Revelation of Witchcraft
The Lord showed Ezekiel a vision the display of witchcraft in the 8th Chapter of Ezekiel from verses 6 through 12:

> *Furthermore He said to me, "Son of man, do you see what they are doing, the great abominations that the house of Israel commits here, to make Me go far away from My sanctuary? Now turn again, you will see greater abominations." So He brought me to the door of the court; and when I looked, there was a*

hole in the wall. Then He said to me, "Son of man, dig into the wall"; and when I dug into the wall, there was a door. And He said to me, "Go in, and see the wicked abominations which they are doing there." So I went in and saw, and there—every sort of creeping thing, abominable beasts, and all the idols of the house of Israel, portrayed all around on the walls. And there stood before them seventy men of the elders of the house of Israel, and in their midst stood Jaazaniah the son of Shaphan. Each man had a censer in his hand, and a thick cloud of incense went up. Then He said to me, "Son of man, have you seen what the elders of the house of Israel do in the dark, every man in the room of his idols? For they say, 'The Lord does not see us, the Lord has forsaken the land.' "

All these revelations shown to God's mighty men of the scriptures are still very much true about witchcraft operations today.

WHAT IS WITCHCRAFT?

Witchcraft is a force of darkness. Witchcraft is the enemy of righteousness. Witchcraft powers are those who eat up people as they eat bread as described in Psalm 53 verses 4b. Witchcraft power is the enforcer of wickedness. Witchcraft power is the embodiment of wickedness. Witchcraft is the author of confusion and deception. Witchcraft is a master manipulator. Witchcraft is the embodiment of evil. Witchcraft is all around; closer than you may think.

HOW REAL IS WITCHCRAFT?

A young lady came for deliverance in church. When she was a little girl, her grandfather gave her witchcraft and all through high school, she was involved in blood magic and sacrificial rituals. We asked her, how did you get into witchcraft?" She said when she was little, her grandfather taught her a lot and wrote her recipes. She said she also had written down notes in unknown languages she could read for rituals. She said while in high school, her best friend confided in her that her father abused her. So she took it upon herself to help her best friend out. She carried out a sacrifice in her best friend's room to empower her best friend. She said immediately the sacrifice was completed, the room became dark for a second, and the reflection of the sun came back into the room. We asked her, what was the outcome? She said the ritual had invoked a bloodthirsty, violent and raging demon into the life of her best friend. She said the girl became so powerful that each time the demon took control of that girl, she would not stop fighting people in school until she broke glasses and drew out blood and injured people. She said she also had the power to extract the demon out of the girl. She said when the demon left the girl, the girl had become shattered, depressed and scattered. And that when she took out the blood, she had to pay back for the needed blood in some ways. She told us that the two times she had been pregnant, she miscarried the babies because there were requirements she needed to pay back with her own blood in the kingdom of darkness. She talked about how there were a lot of younger girls thriving in witchcraft, prostitution and drugs. She said when they begin to see things and hear voices, the doctors think they are schizophrenic and begin to give them doses and doses of drugs which mess up their minds. This was an 18-year old speaking to us. We asked her questions in relation to their processes, and the answers she gave were quite surprising.

Witchcraft is real and terrible, more than we can imagine, and leads to many problems in the school, community, and several places in the society, and in one way or the other, everyone is concerned. There are many young students who are witches ruining destinies, many students who are ruled by terrible demons today.

PREVALENT OCCURRENCE OF WITCHCRAFT

The most common curse that men and women battle with today without knowing it is the curse emanating from witchcraft. If you bring 10 people going through marital issues together, 8 to 9 out of those situations are witchcraft related. When you find 10 people together under terrible financial attacks, it is likely that witchcraft is involved.

When you look for reasons for failure in ministry, witchcraft is likely involved. When you look for reasons behind career death, witchcraft is likely involved. When you look for reasons behind business failures, watch out for witchcraft. Where there is confusion, watch out for witchcraft. When you see interwoven and chain reaction cycles of problems, the spirit of witchcraft is hiding somewhere as the chief sponsor of those problems.

Through witchcraft powers leaders fall, kingdoms are ruined, blood is shed, destinies are disgraced and visions are darkened. By the hands of witchcraft powers, champions become powerless, virtues are swapped, geniuses become nonentities, glories are overturned into rottenness. Through witchcraft powers, people are demoted, people suddenly lose favor, profit suddenly turns loss, helpers become haters, business partners become enemies, marriages turn sour, slumbering churches split up, businesses die, children rebel, finances go south, cities become polluted and the list goes on.

Witchcraft is darkness hidden in plain sight. Witchcraft smiles on the surface, and kills on the inside. Witchcraft specializes in turning colorful destinies into foul-odors. Witchcraft specializes in cutting lives short, and anything related to gross wickedness is witchcraft.

Many Christians are able to perceive bewitchment from afar, only a very few christians are able to enter into the realm where the power of God and His revelation is abundant over their lives to detect the witchcraft operation within their own lives. That is because the nature of witchcraft is concealment, emotional manipulation and deception. God's children who reject satanic ways of manipulation are the ones who can uncover deeper revelations and become victorious warriors by the power in the name of Jesus.

The exceeding greatness of the power of God and the working of His mighty power is availed to us as Christians. This same power is the power that resurrected Jesus from the dead and brought Him into the heavenly places at the right hand of God. There is no doubt that the believer who believes is filled with the power of God that is beyond description. There is a vital task that the believer is being given that is often ignored or overlooked. The burdensome task of standing against the cunningness, craftiness, deceit and schemes of the enemy.

PRAYERS TO DECODE WITCHCRAFT

1. Revelation of the Lord Jesus, expose and disgrace the gathering of emitters and wasters over my life in the name of Jesus
2. No longer shall I be a companion of witches in the name of Jesus
3. Relationships detrimental to my purpose, fire of those relationships, be snuffed out by the fire of the Holy Ghost, in the name of Jesus.
4. Association of witchcraft in my network, be revealed to me by the blood of Jesus, in the name of Jesus.
5. Let the revelation of our Lord Jesus Christ unseal every witchcraft power troubling my life in the name of Jesus.
6. Let the revelation power of the Lord Jesus Christ bring into the open every witchcraft activity against my destiny in the name of Jesus.
7. My God of revelation, open up my eyes in the name of Jesus to hear from you in the name of Jesus.
8. My God of revelation, open up my ears to hear from you in the name of Jesus.
9. My God of revelation, open up all my senses to hear from you in the name of Jesus.
10. Father, as you open up to me, I will not act outside of your word, but I hide in your name in the name of Jesus.

11. Father, open up unto me, deeper secrets in the name of Jesus.

12. Father, reveal unto me the mystery of your power in the name of Jesus.

13. Witchcraft covers around me, is exposed by the finger of God in the name of Jesus.

14. Hidden Witchcraft in my household, be opened in the name of Jesus.

15. Hidden witchcraft in my foundation be exposed in the name of Jesus

16. Hidden witchcraft activities against my health, be exposed and destroyed in the name of Jesus

17. Hidden witchcraft activities against my marriage, be exposed and destroyed in the name of Jesus.

18. Hidden witchcraft in my marriage, be exposed and destroyed in the name of Jesus.

19. Witchcraft hands over my life is exposed and cut off in the name of Jesus.

20. The veil of witchcraft, be torn off by the fire of the Holy Spirit in the name of Jesus.

21. I shall not be initiated into witchcraft in the name of Jesus.

22. I shall not enter into a witchcraft contract, knowing or unknowingly in the name of Jesus.

23. Lord, anoint my eyes with power, that I shall not be bewitched in the name of Jesus

24. Lord, anoint my ears with your power, that I shall not be bewitched in the name of Jesus.

25. Lord, anoint my mind with your power, that I shall not be bewitched in the name of Jesus

26. Lord Jesus, anoint my lips with your power, that I shall not be bewitched in the name of Jesus.

27. Lord Jesus, anoint my feet with your power, that I shall not be bewitched in the name of Jesus

28. Lord Jesus, anoint my mind with your power, that I shall not be bewitched in the name of Jesus.

29. Lord Jesus, anoint my body with your power, that I shall not be bewitched in the name of Jesus.

30. Lord, anoint my senses with your power, that my senses shall not be bewitched in the name of Jesus.

NOTES

2

~

DISBANDING THE ORGANIZATION OF WITCHCRAFT

Witchcraft operation is a robust strategy of the organization of darkness. It is one of the highest organized invisible establishments in the kingdom of darkness. Witchcraft establishments engage in detailed planning, and continue to enlist agents to executive their missions. Witchcraft operation will not advance if the day-to-day assigned tasks of witchcraft agents are unable to be executed. Witchcraft assignments are so complex that the task is broken down into manageable levels. Hardly does witchcraft suddenly destroy a person without succeeding in the previous stages.

WITCHCRAFT OPERATIONS

Everywhere around us, in our communities, in businesses, churches, families, marriages, schools and everywhere thinkable, there is an underground witchcraft operation running. Unfortunately, most of these operations run efficiently too because believers are unaware of them. Witchcraft operations run on a cycle, and this segment breaks down that cycle.

Witchcraft Operations: Demonic Meetings, Demonic Locations, Demonic Agents and Demonic Agendas

Witchcraft establishments run operations like physical establishments that are goal oriented. They have quotas, they have agents, they have targets, they have run strategies and they run meetings all the time. Some of these demonic groups meet every night at specific locations invisible to the eye. Witchcraft operations run everywhere around the world. The downside to this is that their operations are highly guarded one.

Witchcraft Operations: How Witchcraft Operations Run

When witchcraft identifies a mission or a potential victim, the success of that witchcraft operation is organized into multiple levels.

Devices of Witchcraft

Manipulation → Pity → Control → Enslave → Steal → Drain → Kill → Destroy

Witchcraft progresses through each stage of operation only if an individual permits it. A lot of times, witchcraft attacks succeed in the lives of people because of what people allow into their lives. A lot of people find out they have been under witchcraft attacks, but they cannot see the root causes.

Manipulation is a starter tool for witchcraft. Witchcraft cannot function without its agent successful in their manipulation games. This has always been the way of satan from the beginning. Witchcraft does not begin operations in a person's life until the person has allowed themself to be manipulated. After surrendering to the tool of manipulation, witchcraft commences activity in a person's life. Many men, especially the married men fall to the devices of manipulation before they are captured into witchcraft nests. A witchcraft agent pretending to need help manipulates the mind of a naive man. She needs his attention, she needs to enter his mind and take control. She must be able to successfully manipulate to get started.

How to Deal with Witchcraft if You are Currently Being Manipulated

Witchcraft operates in stages. Depending on what stage the witchcraft afflicting you is at, you can unleash God's fire upon that power. You must first recognize the stage. If you are being manipulated, you can be easily delivered at this stage before this power proceeds to the next stage. Witchcraft may seek to manipulate you to give what you don't have. A mother-in-law working under witchcraft spirits attempting to come and live with you in your marriage may seek to manipulate you.

Witchcraft spirits say, "if you do not allow me, or if you do not do this, life will come to an end".

Symptoms of the Trap of Manipulation

1. Witchcraft spirit individual feeds you with lies, to alter your belief systems or truth of a thing, or to change your perspective.
2. You are being manipulated with too much talk that you cannot figure out the truth by yourself, or you hardly can look out for the truth .
3. The witchcraft spirit wears you out with unending conversation to weary your soul.
4. Witchcraft spirits presents you with polluted information, images to bring murky waters into your soul and chase you away from God's presence
5. You may feel defiled after lengthy conversations with these powers

Ending Witchcraft Manipulation

1. *Take back your mind with the Word of God*

2. Never offer the help that will risk your destiny.
3. The solution is never to bow to witchcraft demands.
4. Pray: Pray aggressively the following prayers

Prayers to Rain Down God's Fire
1. Fire of God, deliver me from the arrows of manipulation in the name of Jesus.
2. I set the perimeter made with the fire of God around my mind, in the name of Jesus.
3. My mind, you are not susceptible to the manipulations of darkness in the name of Jesus.
4. The chains of manipulation shall not catch me, in the name of Jesus.
5. My feet shall not be caught in the trap of manipulation in the name of Jesus.
6. My head shall not bow to the manipulations of darkness in the name of Jesus.

Pity is a form of manipulation. The spirit of witchcraft uses this tool a lot to appeal to people's emotions. Getting into the chains of witchcraft pity has ruined many destinies. The chain of pity is used to tie up witchcraft pity. The spirit of witchcraft will position itself disadvantaged so people will show pity. Anyone who is caught in that chain has been hooked. There are many witchcraft agents on the streets disguising as people in need. When people are not able to distinguish the ones in need and the witches, and they give money to the wrong ones, at the close of day, they gather all their money into the coven, to afflict them financially, and people begin to wonder where chronic poverty came through. This began with pity.

Pity is one of the ways of witchcraft. When the spirit succeeds after manipulation, pity is offered back in return. We have been privileged to minister to pastors who have fallen prey. Way back in 2017, there was a sister whom the Lord spoke to through a Word of prophecy during one of our worship sessions. The Lord was calling her to disengage from sexual promiscuity and come into a lifestyle of purity. She stopped coming to our worship gathering, and attempted to discredit the prophecy saying, "What kind of word is that?". Later she said it looks like she found a husband in another church. Within a few months, we found that the "husband" she found was a married pastor, whom they both were having affairs with, and the pastor eventually ran away with this sister. This is nothing other than the works of witchcraft. This individual worked in deep witchcraft, and her devices worked only when she succeeded in manipulation and pity. The pastor in question was one whom the Lord was using greatly, but was defeated by this strange woman.

There was the story of another lady who lost everything she had in a tornado. There was nothing left and nowhere to go. Another lady who was an old schoolmate saw her at the bus stop on a very cold day and picked her up. The lady took her home, they had dinner and she said she had nowhere to go. The lady said, you cannot stay because my husband will soon come", knowing that her husband would not agree to any sleepover arrangement. When the husband came in, to the wife's surprise, the husband said it was okay to stay till morning. By the time it was morning, the husband began to fight with the wife that the lady should be allowed to stay with them till she found a place. This lady began to sleep in their bed, and the wife was chased out. This is the careful work of witchcraft. The spirit of witchcraft positions itself as innocent and naive in front of its victims to gain control.

How to Deal with Witchcraft if You are Have Been Captured in the Stage of Pity

Pity is a major chain of witchcraft to lock people down. Witchcraft spirits are responsible for making people pity an individual who manipulates you. They make you feel bad for not going out of your way to offer help you cannot afford. They guilt trip you for not helping out pay bills, lend them money, or the strange man guilt trip that woman for not paying his bills, or having sex with him, or the strange woman guilt trips the man for saying No to her advances. When you begin to fall into pity, this is a point of no return and you need to call upon the name of the Lord and His fire to deliver you from the snare you are about to enter.

Symptoms of the Trap of Pity
1. You feel you are being arm-twisted
2. You are being guiltripped into an emotional, mental, financial, sexual responsibility that is not yours.

3. You are being guilt-tripped for not giving enough time to engage in senseless manipulation
4. Witchcraft spirits says you have no love when you refuse to bow or be caught in the pity trap

Ending Witchcraft Pity Games

1. *Look into God's Word to see what the Scripture says about that subject and follow through. Do not compromise*
2. *Set a strong defense with fiery prayers around your mind and your soul .*
3. *Never bow to the pity demands, it is a trap*
4. *Pray: Pray aggressively the following prayers*

Prayers to Rain Down God's Fire upon the Witcrhaft Snares of Pity

1. *Fire of God, deliver me from all snares of pity set for my soul, in the name of Jesus*
2. *Fire of God, burn to ashes the devices of pity sent to catch my soul, in the name of Jesus.*
3. *Fire of God, disgrace and destroy the works of darkness all around me in the name of Jesus.*
4. *Fire of God, consume the powers of darkness sent to cage my destiny in the cage of darkness in the name of Jesus.*
5. *I shall not bow to the manifestations of witchcraft pity, in the name of Jesus.*

Control: The next line of item in the witchcraft is operation after successfully winning the war of pity. A witch who has successfully taken over a marriage begins to control the decisions of the primary couples in the marriage. A witch who has successfully taken over a church begins to control what the pastor must say on the pulpit. A witch who has successfully taken over an organization begins to dictate how the CEO leads. Many of those who have fallen victim fearfully submit to the dictates of witchcraft. They become unexplainably influential, and influences against the will and desires of the Lord. Witchcraft goes into a place to attempt to reorganize the order of God in places. Unfortunately, if believers allow witchcraft to enter through manipulation, witchcraft already gains the power to control.

There was the lady who needed deliverance. Her mother-in-law was supposed to visit just for 1 month after they had a baby. She ended up living with them and refused to live. She manipulated them into staying longer, they ended up pitying her, and eventually she took over the control of the marriage. Whenever the wife stepped into the kitchen to cook for her husband, she said, "you do not know how to cook for my son". She took over that family, and suddenly, the man refused to eat when his wife cooked. This is one of the manifestations of bewitchment. After the spirit has taken over the family, it turns itself into an object of pity, and begins to control.

Many are under the control of witchcraft and they do not know it. Whoever falls under witchcraft control, eventually falls into slavery, because witchcraft becomes the master, and the end goal is to drain all virtues out of people until people are destroyed.

How to Deal with Witchcraft if You are Have Been Captured in the Stage of Control

When a person has been captured in the stage of witchcraft control, hardly will they know it. At the stage of witchcraft control, those who are bewitched do not understand what they are doing, they just feel that their lives cannot move forward without the person through which witchcraft is manifesting. There is a solution - intercessors. God uses intercessors around them, family, spouses or children who hold spiritual authority to deliver them from witchcraft control.

Symptoms of the Trap of Control
1. *Another woman or man has taken over your spouse.*
2. *Your spouse suddenly moves out of the house and elopes with a coworker.*
3. *A strange woman takes over the life of a pastor, and the pastor can no longer share the pure Word of God.*
4. *A promising child becomes rebellion or flees from home*

Ending Witchcraft Witchcraft Control
1. *Never confront a witchcraft agent. If you do, they will war against you and change their strategies.*
2. *Never fight an individual who is under witchcraft control physically.*
3. *When you fight them, you fuel and strengthen the witchcraft control powers against the person's soul.*
4. *Make a list of all the manifestations of control. Find examples below:*
    a. *The individual has fled home*

    b. The Individual no longer listens or wants to hear the Word of God. Their spiritual life has been drained

5. After you have finished making a list of the manifestations of control, bring all these items into God's presence to rain down fire on these manifestations and the chain will break

Prayers to Rain Down God's Fire upon the Witcraft Snares of Control

1. Fire of God, come down upon the life of (mention name of bewitched individual) for deliverance in the name of Jesus.
2. Fire of God, deliver (mention name of bewitched person) from witchcraft manifestations.
3. Fire of God, deliver (mention name of bewitched person) from witchcraft control devices in the name of Jesus.
4. Fire of God, deliver (mention name of bewitched person) from witchcraft lockup in the name of Jesus.
5. Fire of God, deliver (mention name of bewitched person) from witchcraft covens in the name of Jesus.
6. Fire of God, deliver the head of (mention name of bewitched person) from witchcraft lockdown in the name of Jesus.

Enslave → Steal → Drain → Kill → Destroy

From the state of control to the state of destruction, witchcraft powers seek to devour the lives of their captives. A husband who runs away from home under witchcraft control will eventually be led into the path of no return. Once control occurs, it is easy for witchcraft to enslave, steal and destroy souls. Many people once captured under the control of witchcraft are enslaved with drug addiction, alcohol, or other agents of ojects of slavery desiged to introduce death slowly. This is always the devil's end game.

WITCHCRAFT CATEGORIES

An active member of a witchcraft group, with spiritual powers, travels into witchcraft meetings and performs rituals. The purpose of this category is to use satanic powers to alter the plans of God for a person. The Scripture below shares more:

#1 ACTIVE WITCHES

Isaiah 47: 5-9 NKJV

"Sit in silence, and go into darkness,O daughter of the Chaldeans;For you shall no longer be called The Lady of Kingdoms. I was angry with My people;I have profaned My inheritance,And given them into your hand.You showed them no mercy; On the elderly you laid your yoke very heavily.And you said, 'I shall be a lady forever,'So that you did not take these things to heart, Nor remember the latter end of them."Therefore hear this now, you who are given to pleasures,Who dwell securely,Who say in your heart, 'I am, and there is no one else besides me;I shall not sit as a widow,Nor shall I know the loss of children';But these two things shall come to you. In a moment, in one day: The loss of children, and widowhood.They shall come upon you in their fullness. Because of the multitude of your

> sorceries, For the great abundance of your
> enchantments.

1. Every work of the flesh is present in the life of an active witch, though they mostly do well to hide these behind a mask, and for believability, some of them hide under "ministry".
2. Active witches work under a strict protocol and mission.
3. Their missions are wicked and destructive in nature. They are given missions to pollute a community, to ensure that a community lives waywardly, to ensure confusion is set in motion in a church, to ensure an individual is derailed from destiny, to ensure that people live in poverty, to ensure that people live in sickness, to ensure that marriages do not stand, to ensure that true ministers of God fall out of God's presence, and the list continues. These are some of the wicked missions of witchcraft.
4. People living in active witchcraft have wicked spirits ruling over them, and all they seek to do is wickedness.
5. Active witches are the ones who carry witchcraft devices around to wreak havoc wherever they go.
6. Active witches will seek to block ways for their captives to hear the word of God or attend a Holy-Ghost charged church.
7. Active witches will drag their captives into churches where the spirit of God is not present, and even assume the role of a minister in those

places to keep their spouses under their bondage permanently.

8. Active witches will seek to lure captives out of hot prayers and fasting, to prevent their captives from entering into God's presence.

9. Active witches sometimes tell their captives, "why are you stressing yourself to pray like this, all these things are not real" to prevent them from being exposed.

10. Active witches are sometimes the most respected, trusted and loyal confidants.

11. Active witches go to church to invite people into covens disguised as membership clubs. They will even name their coven names from the Scripture to cover up (Sister Deborah and Sister Hanna Women's Club).

12. Active witches are sometimes assigned to people to become their best of friends forever. Their main job is to continue to discourage and lead their captives away from purpose.

13. Active witches are sent to lure men of destiny and women of purpose into marriage, so they could ruin their destinies for life.

14. Active witches are sent to ruin thriving communities with sex, pollution, nudity, prostitution, alcohol etc.

15. Active witches mock lukewarm christians and ridicule them a lot.

16. Active witches mock preachers without the fire of God in them.

17. Active witches do join prayer warriors meetings in some churches, and they lead prayers.

18. Active witches do form associations within some church settings, and they seek to hinder the way of holiness in churches.
19. Active witches and the aggressive spirit of poverty is closely knitted.

The list is endless. These are some of the confessions of witches the Lord brought us ministries encounters while ministering to people who are active witches.

#2 WITCHCRAFT OPERATORS

Witchcraft operators are those who participate in the operation of witchcraft through the works of the flesh. Because manipulation is a tool of the enemy, anyone who lies, or slanders, who spreads false reports, or who tries to altar the judgment of other people against the truth is a witchcraft operator. A witchcraft operator cannot successfully battle against witchcraft operations within their own lives because they help further the operations of witchcraft. These can be transient vessels who loan themselves to the devil for use.

John 8:44 NKJV

You are of your father the devil, and the desires of your father you want to do. He was a murderer from the beginning, and does not stand in the truth, because there is no truth in him. When he speaks a lie, he speaks from his own resources, for he is a liar and the father of it.

---

1. The ones who work in jealousy and envy, and pull down with their mouth the work of God in the life of others are witchcraft operators.
2. The ones who live under the yoke of seduction and seek all avenues to sleep with people they are not married to are witchcraft operations, helping to further the mission of witchcraft to cause pollution.
3. The employee who spread rumors in the organization is a witchcraft operator, helping to further the mission of witchcraft to bring down an entire organization.
4. The spouse who manipulates the other is a witchcraft operator, helping further the mission of witchcraft to pull down a marriage.
5. People who are witchcraft operators may be church-goers, but they are highly susceptible to witchcraft influence.
6. Witchcraft operators are the first set of people that active witches usually influence into the overall witchcraft agenda. For example, if an active witch has been sent to tear apart a thriving community, the active witch looks for a person prone to witchcraft influence, such as one who gossips, and begins to influence this individual. Very soon, the witchcraft operator will be the one broadcasting the voice of witchcraft.
7. Witchcraft operators are people who have not had the original salvation experience though they might have been in church for ages.
8. Witchcraft operators are people whom the devil makes use of their tongues a lot.

9. Some witchcraft operators are used to prevent their captives from entering into God's presence. They claim to like a "God-fearing man" or "God-fearing woman", but they will never allow their spouses to truly worship God.
10. Some witchcraft operators are leaders or ministers who have opened themselves up for satanic use.
11. Witchcraft operators are people who have no guard over their mind because witchcraft powers can easily take over their mind to fulfill their assignment.
12. Witchcraft operators are unsteady souls, and are used to further the agenda of witchcraft.

#3 BEWITCHED PEOPLE

Bewitched individuals are everyday people. Apostle Paul said in Galatians 3:1, "*O foolish Galatians! Who has bewitched you that you should not obey the truth, before whose eyes Jesus Christ was clearly portrayed among you as crucified?*".

One of the indicators of bewitchment is that a bewitched person never obeys the truth or listens to the voice of reason. Their mind is locked up and they never know it. They could be the most dangerous types of people to deal with when you are warring against witchcraft. Bewitched people are like the messengers who carry out the assignment of witchcraft without knowing it. They can be people you love, but they have been infiltrated and they are currently held as slaves by witches.

Most marriages where you have a spouse cheating is because the spouse is bewitched. In their right mind, they would not do it. One of the ways you identify a bewitched person is through their speech and actions.

In one of our earlier days in ministry, the Lord revealed with multiple confirmations an individual who worked deep and active witchcraft. Unfortunately, they bewitched a brother who was naive. Now the brother did not know he was under bewitchment, and what they used him for was as a tool to penetrate the places they could not go. They sent him on errands he did not know he was running for witchcraft.

- A bewitched person will get into debts to pay the bills of others.
- A bewitched person will act irrationally, and are at high risk when it comes to making decisions.
- A bewitched person is always used to wreak havoc and made as the scapegoat

Bewitched Objects
The enemy is also crafty enough to bewitch objects that people carry. When objects are bewitched, they can bring in the demons of bad luck, infirmity, poverty, contention and division into people's lives, homes and marriages. When witchcraft powers are unable to locate individuals, they target people's items for bewitchment.

PRAYERS TO EXPOSE WITCHCRAFT ACTIVITIES

Extol the name of the Lord with these powerful lyrics, knowing that no power can stand against the power of . By worshiping the Lord, you are igniting an altar that no witchcraft power can fight or confront.

Lyrics : Find music lyrics on www.ebenezergabriels.org
Yahweh.
Yahweh eh
Yahweh eh
You are Yahweh
that's who You are

Medidate:
Hebrews 12:19 - For our God is a consuming fire.

1. My God is a consuming fire, let all witchcraft fires be consumed in the name of Jesus.
2. My Father, the Keeper of secrets, open unto me every secrets concerning my life in the name of Jesus

3. My Father, the Keeper of secrets, open unto me every secret I need to know for my life to move forward in the name of Jesus.

4. Father, reveal unto me, the witchcraft operations around me in the name of Jesus.

5. My Father, your word says you are a Consuming Fire, therefore start a fire in my life that would consume all witches within and without in the name of Jesus.

6. My Father, disorganized the highly organized witchcraft powers fighting me by your fire in the name of Jesus.

7. My Father, expose and disband the army of witches laying low around me in the name of Jesus with your unquenchable fire in the name of Jesus.

8. My Father, burn down with your fire the shelters and covers of witchcraft powers tormenting my life in the name of Jesus.

9. My Father, rain down fire upon every concealed witchcraft

10. Elaborate schemes of witchcraft against my destiny, be disgraced and destroyed in the name of Jesus

11. Archives of witchcraft against my life, catch fire in the name of Jesus.

12. Father, be my shield and buckler in the name of Jesus

13. My Father, be with me every step of the way, do not leave me or forsake me in the name of Jesus.

14. Carefully concealed Judas in my network, let the finger of God expose them, and lead them into irrecoverable errors unto destruction in the name of Jesus

15. Carefully concealed household wickedness, wreaking havoc in the core of my being, let the right hand of God expose them and destroy them in the name of Jesus.

16. Father, deliver me from all forms of bewitchment targeted at my soul, in the name of Jesus.

17. My spouse shall not be bewitched, in the name of Jesus.

18. My household shall not be bewitched. in the name of Jesus.

19. My marriage shall not be bewitched, in the name of Jesus.

20. The works of my hand shall not be witched, in the name of Jesus.

21. Fire of God, burn to ashes the devices of bewitchment targeted at my life in the name of Jesus.

22. Fire of God, burn to ashes the devices of bewitchment planted in my household, in the name of Jesus.

23. Fire of God, consume the powers of witches sent to capture my soul, in the name of Jesus.

24. Fire of God, rain down brimstone upon the witches and wizards assigned to bring my destiny down in the name of Jesus.

25. Fire of God, rain down brimstone upon the mask of witchcraft hiding to afflict me in the name of Jesus.

26. Fire of God, rain down brimstone upon the hideout of witchcraft hiding to afflict me in the name of Jesus.

27. Fire of God, rain down brimstone upon the enchantment of witchcraft used against me in the name of Jesus.

28. Fire of God, rain down brimstone upon the habitation of witchcraft deciding my case in the name of Jesus.

29. Fire of God, rain down fire and brimstone upon the altar of witchcraft bearing my name in the name of Jesus.

30. Consuming fire of God, rain down the fire of wrath and destruction upon the witchcraft altars where witches are gathered to afflict my destiny, in the name of Jesus.

31. Consuming fire of God, shut down every portal of witchcraft admitting witches into satanic meetings to discuss against my destiny in the name of Jesus .

32. Consuming fire of God, burn down all witchcraft transportation devices against my destiny in the name of Jesus.

33. Consuming fire of God, burn down all witchcraft counsel devices against my destiny in the name of Jesus.

34. Consuming fire of God, burn down all witchcraft monitoring devices against my destiny in the name of Jesus.

35. Lord, deliver me from the chains of witchcraft in the name of Jesus.

NOTES

3

~

WITCHCRAFT MANIFESTATIONS

Certain manifestations can help you decode witchcraft activities around you. Witchcraft manifests in different areas. Many people are naive but when you understand some of the manifestations, you can quench the fiery darts of this dark power.

Proximity: Where there is witchcraft manifestation, witchcraft powers have successfully penetrated a place, or a person's life. The heavier the oppression, the closer witchcraft activities are to you. When there is unexplainable oppression of any kind: spiritual, health, financial, mental or oppression of any sort, witchcraft may be responsible. Sometimes people fast extensively and pray hard, but there are no results. One of the common reasons is that there is a witch close by who is riding on the proximity to you and using that against you. Witchcraft attacks are more potent with proximity, this is why witches look for all avenues to "stop by", "visit", "party", or "hang out" with their victims, just to keep reintroducing affliction after their victim prays them off with prayer. They look for ways to reintroduce affliction through contact. Unfortunately, many believers are non-discerning, and some will fast and pray, but they will never be careful to observe what the Lord iis showing them or calling their attention to.

We were ministering to a man, and the Lord said, **"he is the one using his money to sponsor the witches fighting against him, and that is why the war against him is so potent, because the witches are ensuring that they are using his sweat against him, hence they collect his money to go to purchase recipe from the coven to afflict him"**. Such a wicked world. This is what proximity and access does.

Many people are born out of satanic ancestry. However, they can be fighting the wrong fight because while they are busy targeting the attacks from their village or their grandparents' times; hardly would they ever believe their parents or spouses or children may have entered into witchcraft covenants, and affliction is coming from right under the roof.

We were ministering to a man whose finances was under a rare type of lockdown. God said, **"I am the One calling his attention to this battle. This battle is very close to him. Tell him it is close to home, and he needs to fight it now, and if he does not go deep in prayer, they will derail him and lure him out of prayer"**. He began to pray, soon after he began, he called and said, "I thought it was a big deal, but it wasn't, what I thought was a problem was not". The witches around him had carefully deceived him, and the Lord said, **"they unlocked him a little bit for**

him to have some fresh breath of air, and get him to stop the fasting and prayer, so they can deal with him at a better time when he's relaxed".

Mask: Witchcraft is masked, and witchcraft will do anything to stay masked. This is why they cover up with situations that bring credibility to them. They mostly common coverup with words like, "I have been in the church for 40 years", "I have been a Deaconess for 32 years", and so on. A very common mask they wear these days is the mask of "ministry", knowing that people often associate things of ministry to God, without knowing they are talking about witchcraft ministry. The devil uses this to deceive people and assigns witches to go to Church gatherings to catch souls. They cover up for something major going on underneath. Witchcraft thrives in darkness, and they succeed as long as their activities are hidden, and their agents are undetected. The moment their cover is unveiled, they flee. d

Surveillance: Witchcraft tracks its victims. They torment and monitor people under torment. This is why it is hard for people to slip off their grip, except the Lord snatches His children away. Witchcraft is a highly connected organization. Sometimes, the satanic institution which witches begin to assign more than 1 witch to watch an individual they are working on. Hence, witchcraft surveillance are sometimes people you confide most in, telling them about the dreams you had the previous night. Telling them the job interviews you are attending next. Sometimes they use human surveillance and add double-lay surveillance by placing spiritual trackers on people such that they get into people's dreams, monitor dream lives, and everything people do.

Codependency: Behind every codependent relationship is witchcraft spirit. It is a form of spiritual chain witchcraft uses. The spirit of witchcraft through witches becomes codependent on their victim, such that their victims are enslaved. There are many relationships, parent-to-child, when the child is about to find a husband or a wife, the mother falls sick, and the entire family spends their time resources on the mother's health, and everyone gives all their emotional strength to the sick mother. The mother gets well until the next good thing is about to happen to her son or daughter.

There was an old woman who was usually sick, and the child had to cater for her. The child brought them for prayers. God said, **"she has donated the virtues of the child that brought her, including the child's marriage"** Yet the child does not know that her major marital enemy is her mother whom she takes around for prayers. This spirit becomes codependent on their victims and drains the physical, mental and emotional strength of their victims. For example; to keep her entire family under bondage, a wife under the spirit of witchcraft may pretend to be in an helpless situation needing the emotional, physical, strength of others, which is in turns waste such that she drains them out.

Poverty, Infestation and Desolation: Witchcraft operations can program infestation into a place. They can bring desolation and dilapidation along. Where there is uncontrollable infestation of insects in a house, this is one of the symptoms of witchcraft activity around that home.

People spend money on taking care of a place, and the place continues to degenerate, there is a high possibility witchcraft is at work and no amount of money will regenerate the place until you deal with the witchcraft.

Spiritual Theft: When people do not experience spiritual growth, or where people are experiencing leakage of spiritual power, there is witchcraft close. Witchcraft agents steal from spiritual power by luring people into lifestyles that are non-compatible to the way of the Holy Spirit.

Disease-Planters: Witchcraft specializes in planting illnesses in people. Sometimes, people find out that their things are missing, and suddenly they find it back at later times and were thinking they did not know where it was placed. When you constantly have missing items, watch out more. Witchcraft agents steal things from people's houses, take them to the coven for rituals on it and return it back to harm the victims. Many of those items, if they are worn back, introduce chronic illnesses into people's bodies.

There are a lot of caregivers who are the witches eating up the health of those they are caring for. The Lord said to tell an individual, "**your caregiver is not your god. Tell her to stop coming**``.The individual fought hard saying she cannot even do anything by herself until this satanic nurse came. She was so sick that she waited for the nurse to even hand her a glass of water. Suddenly in the middle of it, she said to the caregiver, "do not come tomorrow", and the moment the caregiver stopped, she experienced life again, and all the diseases vanished. God said the nurse was used as an entry of darkness to continue pumping infirmities into that individual.

Marriage Destructions: When you see people behave foolishly in a marriage, where men begin to cheat on their wives, become addicted to late night calls, hangout, there is likely the operation of witchcraft at work.

Witchcraft and Lies

Witchcraft agents come to check out ministers all the time to measure your level of discernment. There is no church where there is no witch. That's correct. There is no church where a witch is not assigned to. Some of them are very dedicated workers that if care is not taken, they will stay detected for years until they ruin the anointing and desecrate the altar. Some of them will bring elaborate lies to draw out pity during counseling, if a minister is not able to discern, they will present you with lies. And those ministers will pray the wrong prayers and even fall to the wrong side of God. Witchcraft spirits can place a church and the ministers there under curses if they are not dealt in a timely manner.

Witchcraft and Commitments

Witchcraft agents come around people and especially in the Church to sign demonic contracts. They come to ensnare people with words, with demonic covenants. In African Churches, a lot of them come under the cover of they are celebrating some event and bring an Aso-Ebi (*a type of fabric design where everyone should wear to an event signifying membership to the same cause/friendship group/club*) for people to buy; as many as buy those clothes get into trouble. We prayed for a lady whom the

Lord said some people will bring some clothes for your buy-in for a party, they are trying to bring you into their demonic group. She said they already gave her the clothes in a Church group and payment was pending.

PRAYERS TO EXTINGUISH WITCHCRAFT POWERS

Extol the name of the Lord with these powerful lyrics, knowing that no power can stand against the power of . By worshipping the Lord, you are igniting an altar that no witchcraft power can fight or confront.

Lyrics : Find music lyrics on www.ebenezergabriels.org
Sabaoth Sabaoth Lord of Host
Elohim Adonai
King of kings
Let my life
before you be
All my days
in your court
To Your Leading
I submit
Your Presence
I approach
Draw me In

Psalm 29:7 - *The voice of the Lord divides the flames of fire.*

1. Let the God who answers by fire expose and consume all witchcraft afflicting me by proximity in the name of Jesus.
2. Let the power which tore down the temple veil from up to bottom tear down all witchcraft masks, veils and covering in the name of Jesus.
3. My Father, Your word says You are the Lover of my soul, therefore let every hater of my soul be crushed by your feet in the name of Jesus.
4. Consuming fire of God, consume every surveillance programs and devices of witches assigned against my life, in the name of Jesus
5. O Fire of God, burn to ashes, the manipulation of witchcraft against my life in the name of Jesus.
6. O fire of God, cast out the spirit of destructive bias out of my life in the name of Jesus.
7. O Fire of God, come into my body, soul, mind in the name of Jesus so that I will not align through the works of flesh against your enemies in the name of Jesus.
8. Lord God of Hosts, arrest every spiritual thief and witches stealing my godly visions in the name of Jesus.
9. Witchcraft arrows of disease fired into my body, I decree by the word of God, thou arrows go back to your senders in the name of Jesus.
10. Witchcraft implantation into my body, be uprooted by the finger of God in the name of Jesus.
11. Witchcraft plantation in my home, be exposed and destroyed by the consuming fire of God in the name of Jesus.

12. Witchcraft plantation in my destiny, be exposed and destroyed by the consuming fire of God in the name of Jesus.
13. I will not end up in the cauldron of darkness, in the name of Jesus.
14. Deliver my destiny from every concealed web of darkness, in the name of Jesus
15. Deliver me from the trap of witchcraft perilous pestilence in the name of Jesus
16. My life will not end up as meat in the cauldron of darkness in the name of Jesus.
17. I reject death in the name of Jesus.
18. My head rejects death in the name of Jesus.
19. Conspiracy of darkness to exchange my destiny, fail and perish in the name of Jesus.
20. Voice of God, exposee all manifestations of witchcraft in the name of Jesus.
21. Voice of God, expose the witchcraft manifesting through proximity in the name of Jesus.
22. Voice of God, destroy the fire of witchcraft targeting my destiny for destruction in the name of Jesus.
23. Voice of God, quench the fire of witchcraft infirmity targeting my health in the name of Jesus
24. Voice of God, quench the fire of poverty against my life in the name of Jesus.

NOTES

4

~

WITCHCRAFT IN THE WORKPLACE

Witchcraft has penetrated into many workplaces today.

Witchcraft in the Workplace (I)

I was in my third year in College; I began applying for internship roles. I had many interviews and during one of those interviews was my first prophetic encounter of witchcraft in the workplace. It was a steel construction company and the company had been in existence for about 20 years. The owners of the company had passed away. The company was once a profitable business but suddenly went into a phase of decline. If the decline was not checked; one thing was certain, they were going out of business. They found out their problems stemmed from toxic employee behavior and people did whatever they liked; and it was impacting their business. During my interview, my interviewer said to me; *"you took a course in leadership and organizational behavior where you designed a change management plan for a consulting organization"* I said yes and gave him details of what I had worked on in that area. Then the interviewer said in a low voice to me *"we need your help, you see those people you saw as you walked through the reception, they have been in this company for long, before the founders passed. They are so toxic to the workplace they do what they like. Are you able to help us fire them?* I said to him, the problem your organization faces may not be resolved by letting go of your current human capital. You may need to train them to help them go through changes in your processes. At this time; I believed I had fresh knowledge of the concepts of organizational behavior and change management which was what the interviewer said they were looking for. The interviewer got disappointed when I mapped out my planned change management process for the company if I was hired. The interviewer who happens to be the general manager of the company seemed to have his mind made up and he was only looking for people who can help him fire the majority of his office staff. I found out that the General Manager would sometimes hide in his office and could not relate with his employees or get them to perform their regular tasks. They were in control and he was looking for ways to get rid of them because he couldn't do it for unknown reasons. He seemed to be scared of them and I found he was working under fear. He never gave me that job; because I recommended a different plan from what he wanted.

Looking back now; I am thankful I never got the job. When the Lord opened my eyes, the organization had been infiltrated by witchcraft. Any new person hired is placed under a spell to conform or initiate. A spiritually immature believer brought into that company would be seriously dealt with if not wasted by these powers. The truth is that I couldn't have effectively applied my knowledge of leadership and organizational behavior without spiritual authority in an environment dominated by witchcraft powers. It turns out that this business was in a witchcraft infested region where no business is allowed to thrive in the spiritual realm. In that zone, many businesses were closed down, and the few ones left opened were petty businesses. This interview was prophetic because it captures a critical part of God's assignment that has long awaited us in ministry today: which is restoring and building worship altars of YHWH and intercession for communities and nations - and in order to do that, wickedness must be uprooted from the foundations.

Witchcraft in the Workplace (II)

Now while in ministry, years after that experience of witchcraft in the workplace as a college student, the Lord gave us another instance of witchcraft in the workplace. A brother was hired into a supervisory role due to his experience and educational background. It was a high-paying job, one that would help meet the needs of his family, pay his children's school fees and upgrade the economy of his home. He was determined to bring his best to the organization and move up the ladder through hard work. He was indeed excited to begin this new job and looking forward to bringing a change to the new organization he had just become a part of. The first day he got to work; he realized that the organization was dealing with employee tardiness. This brother was not only punctual, he was a kind that prefers to be early. From the very first day as a new manager, his first goal was to restore punctuality to the team. On his new team was a younger woman; a seemingly naive woman who operated proficiently in high-level Jezebel and witchcraft spirit. Immediately the brother resumed work; the younger woman became friends with her new boss. The friendship thrived quickly, by his third day on his new job, the brother became biased and defensive of every insubordination committed by the woman at work. By his second week on the job; there was constant communication; voice, video and SMS between the lady and the brother in and out of work. At work, the woman was placed under investigation over workplace non-compliance issues, when the brother was presented with facts and asked for an evaluation; the brother got defensive of the woman. By his second week anniversary on the job, he was fired; and the brother suddenly woke up to reality. How does he explain to his wife that he had just been fired at his new job due to his faithfulness to a strange woman? How does he explain his constant non-work related secret phone calls, video calls with a strange woman to his wife? How does he tell his wife that instead of doing the work he was hired to do, he aligned himself with and defended a non-complying employee? What reason would he give to his children that their hope of getting their next school fees paid had just been cut short? He finds no answers. This once-determined-to-succeed-brother had just gone through bewitchment. Anyone believer who is not deeply planted in Christ could go through the same experience as this brother. He got a well-paying position, intended to be the best at his workplace, but fell into the trap of witchcraft and lost his testimony within two weeks.

WITCHCRAFT SITTING ON BUSINESS SUCCESS

In some workplaces, it is the receptionist, and their job is to ensure that nothing good ever comes into such businesses. There was the case of a receptionist who suddenly resigned because the general manager was a prayerful believer. The receptionist resigned, after the man specifically began to pray to the Lord to move his business forward, and in her resignation, she wrote, "I have to leave so that the company can grow". This is why many businesses do not grow, especially businesses owned by lukewarm believers. Such businesses are the prime target of witches who do their best to ensure such businesses never succeed. They look for loopholes, send their agents to set traps to pull down leaders and destroy missions. Some of them get into strategic roles close to leadership such as Receptionists, Executive Assistants, Personal Assistants, Special Assistants or Human Resources. This is one of the reasons for failure in many businesses.

WITCHCRAFT TAKEOVER IN ORGANIZATIONS

In some companies, they have taken over such that the owner of the company becomes afraid of them. There are business owners who cannot go to their workplace to manage their business anymore because witchcraft has taken over.

There are a lot of unsuspecting business owners they have taken over from. There was a young woman the

Lord brought us in contact with. She was deeply into witchcraft. Her speciality is paralyzing business owners. There was a man living in England with businesses in other countries. She alongside with other witches assigned to that establishment planted infirmity into the man, and he went from one doctor to the other, one surgery to another, while the witch positioned herself as the man's savior who could run the business in his absence. Each time she succeeds, she ensures the business owner is totally wrecked and looks for the next business owner. These are classic examples of witchcraft powers pulling down the strong and mighty in their career, pulling down businesses and organizations who set out to bring change to communities.

OTHER WITCHCRAFT ACTIVITIES IN THE WORKPLACE

Witchcraft powers sometimes spread diseases in the workplace to paralyze team efforts, especially targeting people who are doing well on the job. Suddenly they find out that they have been unusually sick since they started the job, or since someone was brought to join the team. This is one of the activities of witchcraft in the workplace. Witchcraft is the leading cause of career failures. Witchcraft looks for creative ways to pull down organizations, bright employees and their activities are dynamic, the child of God only needs to stay tuned in to the channel of the Holy Spirit to uncover their activities and destroy their powers by the living power of God.

When you have a mass exit in the workplace, this may be a ploy of wickedness. Witchcraft is against profitability in the workplace. At work, they scatter teams, sow dissension, and bring desolation into the workplace.

The goal of witchcraft is to break organizational structure, overturn processes and derail leadership. Keep your organization in prayers.

PRAYERS AGAINST WITCHCRAFT IN THE WORKPLACE

1. Finger of God, shoot back to senders all witchcraft arrows of error fired into my work in the name of Jesus
2. Finger of God, shoot back to senders all witchcraft arrows of failure fired into my work in the name of Jesus.
3. Finger of God, locate, disgrace and destroy all witchcraft powers working hard to discredit me in the name of Jesus
4. Fire of God, consume all witchcraft devices set against me in the name of Jesus
5. Fire of God, consume the witchcraft device of distraction set against me in the name of Jesus
6. Fire of God, consume the witchcraft devices of downfall set against me in the name of Jesus
7. Fire of God, consume all witchcraft powers lurking around to ruin my career in the name of Jesus
8. Fire of God, unseat and consume witchcraft powers seating upon my career advancement in the name of Jesus.
9. Career-eating witchcraft powers, you are consumed by the fire of the Holy Spirit in the name of Jesus.
10. Witchcraft powers planting sicknesses into the workplace, let the light of God expose you and the

fire of God destroy you in the name of Jesus.

11. Every arrow of error fired into my life to kill my career, let the fire of God send those arrows back to devour the senders in the name of Jesus.

12. Arrows of mistake fired into my career destiny,let the fire of God return the arrows back to senders in the name of Jesus. .

13. Arrows of error fired into my brain to disgrace my career, let the fire of God return the arrows back to senders in the name of Jesus.

14. Arrows of error fired into my mouth, let the fire of God return the arrows back to senders in the name of Jesus.

15. Arrows of error fired into my eyes, let the fire of God return the arrows back to senders in the name of Jesus.

16. Witchcraft congregation afflicting my career destiny, let the fire of God consume you to ashes in the name of Jesus.

17. Witchcraft powers sitting upon my promotion, let the fire of the Holy Spirit consume you in the name of Jesus.

18. Witchcraft embargoes my career advancement, devouring fire of God, devouring the powers behind the embargo and the embargo and setting my career free in the name of Jesus.

19. Witchcraft career counselors, assigned to lure me out of career advancement, let your evil counsel be disgraced and destroyed in the name of Jesus.

20. Witchcraft powers, assigned to monitor my career growth, the consuming fire of God puts an end to you in the name of Jesus.

NOTES

4

~

WITCHCRAFT IN THE CHURCH

Witchcraft has crept into the church, and has taken over the control of many churches. In 2016, The Lord said, **"there are a lot of people jumping into hell from the Church because witchcraft has gone to the source, which is the church to cause pollution"**. The Lord said His people who listen will be delivered by the truth of His word. Witchcraft is responsible for many of the churches converted to entertainment centers and dance houses. Witchcraft is the reason why the voices of true worshippers are silenced in the church. Witchcraft is responsible for lack of spiritual growth in churches. Witchcraft is the reason why the spirit of true prophecy is silenced in churches. Unfortunately, many are too blind to see it, and many are too deaf to hear it. This is why people who have been attending a church for years and have never experienced God in a major way will refuse to leave. There is a force tying them down.

WITCHCRAFT IN THE CHURCH (I)

The church is the body of Jesus Christ, the gathering of believers, fellowship of God's people where they are fed spiritually. Heaven releases wisdom to the earth through the Church. All gifts are released and nurtured through the local Church and gifting manifests through God's children as they work in different roles: Musicians, Prophets, Apostles, Evangelists, Teachers and Administrators. This makes the Church the number 1 high target area for witchcraft for the sole reason of polluting the source. Many churches have been taken over by witchcraft. Rather than asking the Holy Spirit what God wants to share with people, Pastors have submitted to witches, and they now have Sermons assigned to witches, and the witches come forth with Coven agenda to hand over to the pastor saying, "this is what you must preach if you want to bring in people".

Witchcraft is one of the first battles every ministry leader will have to confront and overcome for you to advance into what God has called them to do. Unfortunately, many ministers have fallen into the dungeon of witches. A sister invited us to their church. The Lord said, **"I will show you what they are doing on the altar"**. When we got there, the Lord said, **"You see all the ushers, they are all witches, and they are the ones helping the pastor to hold down the crowd, and there are a lot of destinies that have been tied down there"**.

The Lord said, "**In this church, no marriage thrives and people's minds are darkened, as all the men come in, the witches are hugging them and stealing virtues from them**". Right there, the Pastor began to perform, rolling around in his tight-fitted suit and telling the congregation how he got the money to buy his highly-expensive belt, and shoe, and the crowd roared. Some of them got up, and it was dancing time, they began to spray the pastor dollar notes in the head. The Lord said, "**The man's life is in great danger, there is no oil and he is aborting babies for quite a number of ladies**" This is one of the cases of many witchcraft takeover in the church. Many fallen ministers are now working for witches.

SYMPTOMS OF WITCHCRAFT ACTIVITIES IN YOUR CHURCH

1. The word of God is lacking. What is being preached is different from what the Scripture teaches. There is a perversion, or conformity to today's standard or make everyone comfortable with the sermon.
2. There is no move of the Holy Spirit
3. There is no spiritual growth.
4. There is so much oppression around
5. There is no tangible deliverance
6. Your church feels like a social club where all that happens is networking, dining and winning.

Witchcraft agents are sent to bring the church into spiritual ineffectiveness. Witchcraft agents go into the church as the most qualified personnel to give professional suggestions to ministers. Their goal is to deter ministers from building according to the design of God, just as God warned Moses.

Exodus 25:40

See that you make them according to the pattern shown you on the mountain.

They come to suggest in fine ways to men and women of God who are sleeping to build according to satanic patterns. Witches may claim professional marketing expertise to help your ministry grow on the condition that you modify the message and preach more people-friendly messages rather than the authenticity of the gospel of the Lord Jesus. We live in times where it is better to go into fasting and prayer before you go to any church. There are people who plan to test out a church, they go for 1 day, 1 week, 2 months, 5 years, and before they wake up, they've been in the church 30 years, and all their destinies have been emptied. Some people never even recover from ever stepping their foot into some churches. It is the responsibility of every believer to pray to the Lord:

1. Lord, show me the spiritual state of where I am being fed in the name of Jesus.
2. Lord show me what is happening in the Church. Is your presence still here?

INITIATED IN THE CHURCH

We prayed for a lady from Illinois. The Lord said, **"tell her they are going to have her buy some cloth from her church because she is a member of a group where they were organizing an event. Tell her not to participate, it is an initiation into witchcraft the moment she wears that cloth".** She said they had already told her about the clothes and she was waiting for them to bring it. Immediately, she heard what God said, she went ahead to reject the cloth.

A lot of invitations into witchcraft taking place from the church. There are many satanic agents who visit the church, and towards the end of the service, they look around for vulnerable people, and exchange cards, invite them to a cookout, or to a Bible-study over coffee or to a prayer meeting for specific people. Many who say "yes" and go head into the unknown, and have met with greater woes. There was a lady who was a Spa professional, she would wait afterwards, and tell people she wanted to invite people for business from the church, eventually, this lady said she was an Administrative Specialist in a witchcraft group.

There are some ministers who have met their doom in the church too. These are both young and older ministers who have fallen into the trap of witches. Pastor Adam (not real names) was a minister in a congregation where about 7000 worshiped every week. Pastor Adam is one of the many ministers serving under an elderly minister. The elderly minister is an uncompromising servant of God, as a result, the Lord moves powerfully in his ministry. However, due to covetousness, some of the ministers working under him target people seeking counseling, especially women who appear to be perpetually in need of counseling, and position themselves as the best alternative since their boss (the elderly minister) has a packed schedule. Pastor Adam knew how to gently speak to the women, most married, and give them his contact to call him for prayers outside of church. Pastor Adam's living room was his home office. His wife welcomed this arrangement and all sorts of women needing prayers came to their house. Pastor Adam also went to their houses to sanitize the house especially when the women complained they were having bad dreams, or attacks. Most of these women, when they visited Pastor Adam, they brought gifts, groceries and all sorts, just as Jezebel haad the habit of feeding the prophets of Asherah.

---

1 King 18:19
Now summon the people from all over Israel to meet me on Mount Carmel. And bring the four hundred and fifty prophets of Baal and the four hundred prophets of Asherah, who eat at Jezebel's table."

Unknown to Pastor Adam, most of these women were witches who wanted to make a scapegoat of the ministers working under the anointed man of God especially because of the kind of miracles that were happening in his ministry. By the time the witches were done with Pastor Adam, he did not know which of the groceries he ate that was killing his family member one by one, or which of the witches was responsible. All he knew is that his covetousness had invited evil into his life.

Proverbs 7:26-27 NKJV

Many are the victims she has brought down; her slain are a mighty throng. Her house is a highway to the grave, leading down to the chambers of death.

There are many ministers like Pastor Adam who go meet people behind and outside of church protocols. It never ends well.

WHEN WITCHCRAFT IS IN THE ALTAR ALREADY

In some churches, there are witches on the altar already ministering to people, laying hands and feeding people Holy Communion. Many people had no problems until they started attending a witchcraft infested church. They just found that there are multiple problems showing up in their lives but yet they cannot leave. Sometimes, the Lord begins to show them dreams, and they foolishly translate this dream by flesh. We ministered to a lady who was going through severe affliction and the Lord said, "she is drinking from a polluted stream, and His glory cannot be birth forth in her life in a polluted anointing". I told her the vision, and she said, that it is true and she had a dream saying "where are you drinking water from" ?. She was going to a witchcraft-infested church.

Unfortunately, some of the witches are the Pastor, or the Pastor's wife, or the elders, or the choir members or the drummers, or people who hold a high place in the church. For those who receive the Lord's mercy, the Lord will begin to open their eyes, warn them through dreams, some people will be shown what is happening in those places, some people will see themselves in prisons, some will see themselves being tied down around faces they see in church, some people will see themselves working under hard labor in church environments, some people will see their spiritual leader chaining them down, unfortunately, a lot of these people still go to tell report the dreams and visions back to the witches in church, and they lead them into deceptive translation. In such cases, God sometimes keeps quiet and stops revealing to those. For those who can ask God for more, he reveals more and warns them to stay away from such covens.

THE WITCHCRAFT MONITOR IN THE CHURCH

There is no church where witchcraft agents do not attend or visit. Witches attend church regularly even the Holy-Spirit filled church, some of them pay close attention to sermons that some believers do, so they go back to report what the Lord is set to do in the season;

Ephesians 3:10 NKJV
to the intent that now the manifold wisdom of God might be made known by the church to the principalities and powers in the heavenly *places*

People may ask, but why do witches come to Church, or why the Lord allows them in the Church. We must be reminded that the Lord loves everyone, and does not want any soul to perish. *Gracious is the LORD, and righteous; Yes, our God is merciful* - Psalm 116;5 NKJV. Unfortunately, witches hardly repent, even though the Lord gives them an opportunity to hear His word unto salvation. Yet despite God's grace, many witchcraft agents still boldly go into Churches to cause pollution. The Witchcraft spirit hates the true apostolic and prophetic ministry especially the Lord uses the apostolic ministry as a specialized tool to expose and tear down their house of wickedness.

To further divert people from the word of God, witchcraft tries to clone the apostolic and prophetic ministry to paint themselves as anointed men and women of God - when in fact they are anointed of Baal. They prophesy, they lay hands, and are very full of venom. Many people have made major life decisions based on prophecies received from these prophets and prophetesses of Baal.

WITCHCRAFT & DIVINATION

Many people go from place to place seeking prophetic words, and fast miracles, and through this, many have been initiated into witchcraft while some have submitted their destinies. The people who are most prone to witchcraft initiation are the ones who go house to house seeking divination.

Witchcraft agents are sent out to go invite people and invite them to a "prophetic man or woman" for "prayers". The moment people visit, they ask them to partake in strange food and drinks, and problems begin. Some people suddenly begin to see themselves in witchcraft coven, some become suddenly sick, some submit their glory.

A few months ago, the Lord said pray against every cloud of darkness over a region. I was in a parking lot in Maryland, and I heard the Lord say "I want to show you something". Within seconds, I saw a man park in the parking lot where there were no cars or people watching, he got out of his car, opened his trunk, brought out a black suitcase, looked around and released black birds into the air, and the Lord this is a witchcraft effort to lock up the atmosphere of the place.

A brother received a Prophetic word during the February 2020 Worship Unto Deliverance. The Lord said a woman was seated upon his virtues, and this woman appeared to be doing well, but with the use of the brother's glory. Afterwards the brother shared how his previous girlfriend took him to a practicing Nigerian witch in the United States. The first interesting part of his story is that this was the same region where the Lord had called for prayers over the atmosphere. The second interesting part of his story is that he says the lady who took him to see a witch is a "christian who goes to church regularly".

Witches sometimes are the ones taking their captives to different ministries for prayers. We met with an individual for prayers, and the Lord said, the one who brought him is "deep in witchcraft". Many witches take people to even places of God's power, to build trust. Unfortunately, many children of God despite getting nudges and warnings from the Holy Spirit, they still choose to stick with the chief witch ruining their lives, and would sometimes even give glory to them.

Many witches in ministry go in search of prophecies, so they can go broadcast to gain credibility amongst their captives.

Hence, believers must stay focused, and strive for spiritual growth, so that the gifts of the Holy Spirit can be multiplied unto them. Believers must never live in fear, because by inheritance, believers hold high authority through the power of the Lord Jesus, and satanic agents also fear believers for this great privilege. Hence, every believer must know and take their place in Christ.

PRAYERS AGAINST WITCHCRAFT IN THE CHURCH

1. Witchcraft and manipulation, be exposed by the fire of the Holy Spirit in the name of Jesus.
2. Witchcraft committee assigned against the church of God globally, the gates of hell shall not prevail over the church, therefore be exposed in the name of Jesus.
3. Witchcraft agents sent to pollute the call of God over my life, let the flaming sword of the Lord chop you off in the name of Jesus.
4. Witchcraft powers that have spread problems into my life let the fire of the Holy Spirit nullify such powers in the name of Jesus.
5. Virtues that have departed into my life, as a result of submission to witchcraft anointing, let the power of the Holy Spirit anoint me afresh and restore my virtues in the name of Jesus and by the fire of the Holy Ghost.
6. Wickedness that has entered my life places of gatherings disguised as churches, Father, deliver me by the living fire of God in the name of Jesus Lord, have mercy on me and recover every of my

glory I have donated in satanic gatherings in the name of Jesus and by the living fire of God

7. Powers that have placed me in trouble to enjoy life, be disgraced and destroyed by the power in the name of Jesus. I come out of every trouble of life in the name of Jesus and by the fire of God

8. Powers fighting me with curses and enchantments from satanic worship centers, catch fire by the fire of the Holy Ghost in the name of Jesus.

9. Father, if I am a casualty of witchcraft in the church-gathering, Lord deliver me and heal me in the name of Jesus.

10. Witchcraft release of arrows from satanic pulpits, my life is not your landing spot, in the name of Jesus, return back to your senders in the name of Jesus.

11. Father, deliver me from every confusion set in motion by witchcraft voices in the name of Jesus.

12. Father, deliver my portion from the dungeon of wickedness in the name of Jesus.

13. Father, every withered hand that has laid its hand on my glory, let the fire of the Holy Spirit consume those hands in the name of Jesus.

14. Father, let my glory be unburdened from the load placed upon my head through laying off heavy hands with heavy yokes in the name of Jesus.

15. I demolish every witchcraft plan over my destiny in the name of Jesus.

16. Divination against my life, go back to sender in the name of Jesus

17. My Father, break the sorcerer's beam in the name of Jesus.

NOTE

5

~

WITCHCRAFT WITHIN THE FAMILY

In many families today, witchcraft is thriving and many do not know they are battling with witchcraft. The wife manipulates the entire family into her desire. The wife manipulates the emotions of the husband just to have her way. The wife manipulates the children. It may be the reverse, the husband manipulates the entire household. The husband manipulates the children. Remember from chapter 2, manipulation is one of the starter tools of witchcraft. Any form of manipulation is witchcraft. The question is; how deep is the witchcraft you are addressing. In some families, the parents are the ones sacrificing the children. This is strange but it is not new, the Scripture mentions this:

Psalm 106:37-38

They even sacrificed their sons And their daughters to demons, And shed innocent blood, The blood of their sons and daughters, Whom they sacrificed to the idols of Canaan; And the land was polluted with blood.

A lady said her grandfather gave her mother witchcraft, and her mother gave her witchcraft. Witchcraft can be hereditary and also transferable. People pass witchcraft spirits to their children, their siblings, their friends. Some are initiated as soon as they are born by their parents, some are initiated as they grow older. A woman told us that her grandparent initiated her into witchcraft and taught her every ritual she knows. There are mothers initiating their children and there are fathers initiating their children into witchcraft.

WITCHCRAFT: MEMBERS OF THE SAME HOUSEHOLD

Witchcraft is vast, but you can detect it by understanding its nature and by learning to listen to the Holy Spirit. During one of our worship sessions, we were in deep worship and we were on the 2nd hour of worship when the Lord began to speak. The Lord said, "*there is someone here, they have picked a date that they are going to sacrifice you in witchcraft coven, but because you have* come to worship me this morning, instead of you, those who have gone to put your name forward for sacrifice will die instead". Then an individual said someone whom she came to church with, worshiping in the same service, called her to a corner, "excuse me, I want to see you. I am very scared. The lady said," Why are you scared?", and the person told her, "From the message God sent today, they said someone who has gone to donate your name in the coven will die". The lady was panicking after she heard this, because the person who brought her to church to pray was her mother.

WITCHCRAFT: MEMBERS OF THE SAME HOUSEHOLD

Witchcraft within the family is usually a tough one to deal with, especially where there is direct blood relationship. Those who have been bewitched sometimes become biased or emotional, or begin to pity witches. A basic rule that witches know is that when it is the time to strike hot, or when it is their turn to sacrifice in their group, they will sacrifice anyone, whether such people is their husband, wife, son, daughter, sister, brother, regardless of how close they are or how their target has been good to them, they do not care.

There was a very old woman. The Lord said, "**go and tell her, I am giving her grace to come into repentance. She is the one blocking her children's advancement in their witchcraft group**", When I delivered the word, she said, "God is not lying". She began to speak about things they do. She said she had different types of satanic technologies and she used one to bring demons of rage into the home of married couples. She said, whenever she brought the device into a peaceful home, if Jesus is not present, the home is already scattered. Witches do not prioritize relationships. If they are sent to scatter their children's marriage. They just do it, if they are able to..

WITCHCRAFT: MEMBERS OF THE SAME HOUSEHOLD

Many men are married to witches. Some begin to suspect early, but it takes a lifetime for others to figure out. The witches keep many men in ignorance by disguising as Christian prayerful wives, such that the men contract out their prayer lives to their wives. The wife becomes the only one who "sees visions", who "dreams dreams" and who architect the design and plan of the destiny of everyone in the house. The men remain in continual spiritual slumber and never have a tangible experience with the Lord. All hell breaks loose whenever the men attempt to get closer to the Lord, the women lure them out of that encounter subtly.In the coven, such women are sent out against mighty men whom God's design is mighty upon their lives. Unfortunately, a lot of men have fallen prey.

Also there are the men who are the sorcerers, those who have been initiatcd into satanic groups. There was the case of a man who had been initiated into the occult, and the group members were the ones torturing his wife. The Lord said, tell the wife "**to come closer to me and pray hard so they do not waste her**"

There is the case of mother to child, husband to wife, wife to husband, sister to sister and all sorts of dynamic, but it is always common for believers who are deep in God's presence to marvel in disbelief when the Lord reveals those working in witchcraft within the family. Most times, one of the first reactions is that people ask, how can this person turn around or be saved, or how can I pray for them? Witchcraft victims, always hold good intentions, attempt to intercede for the spirit of witchcraft. Most times, witchcraft spirits do not repent, and they get more dangerous over time. Witchcraft within the family is usually a tough one to deal with, especially where there is direct blood relationship. Those who have been bewitched sometimes become biased or emotional, or begin to pity witches. A basic rule that witches know is that when it is the time to strike hot, or when it is their turn to sacrifice in their group, they will sacrifice anyone, whether such people is their father, mother, or twin.

PRAYERS TO EXTINGUISH WITCHCRAFT POWERS WITHIN THE FAMILY

1. By the finger of God, I tear apart the legislation of witchcraft from deep within my ancestry against my life in the name of Jesus.
2. Mask of witchcraft, be shattered by the by the blood of Jesus
3. Witchcraft barbers, scraping my hair in the middle of the night, Father arrests and consumes them in the name of Jesus.
4. Influence of ancestral witchcraft in my life, be exposed and destroyed in the name of Jesus
5. Foundational witchcraft, wiping out my mind into blankness, I am delivered from you by the finger of God, in the name of Jesus.
6. Household witchcraft companions, be exposed and destroyed in the name of Jesus.
7. Works of witchcraft against me from within my bloodline, be exposed and catch fire in the name of Jesus.
8. Powers wanting to use me as a placeholder or replacement in a witchcraft group, catch fire in the name of Jesus.

9. The power of demonic and ancestral witchcraft is broken over my life in the name of Jesus.

10. All the virtues of my destiny stored up in the territory of darkness, be released by the wind of God in the name of Jesus.

11. Items from my body kept from the time I was born in witchcraft safe, let the finger of God set those items free and my destiny is free in the name of Jesus.

12. Hands placed upon my head that is letting my life resist prayers, let those evil hands be cut off in the name of Jesus

13. Water of affliction, be purged out of my life in the name of Jesus

14. Carefully concealed Judas in my network, let the finger of God expose them, and lead them into irrecoverable errors unto destruction in the name of Jesus

15. Carefully concealed household wickedness, wreaking havoc in the core of my being, let the right hand of God expose them and destroy them in the name of Jesus.

16. Satanic network of 7 gathering together against my life, perish by the devouring fire of God

17. Satanic network of 7 congregating together against the manifestation of God's glory in my life , perish by the devouring fire of God in the name of Jesus

18. Witchcraft tactic (mode of oppression) working to suppress the power of God, designed to hinder the move of God in my life, be exposed and disgraced and destroyed in the name of Jesus

NOTES

6

~

WITCHCRAFT &

ADDICTIONS

Witchcraft, unholy sex, drugs, prostitution and all forms of addiction go hand in hand. Witches seek to manipulate and catch their victims, and introduce a form of addiction as a hook. Witches study people's weaknesses and tendencies. Some people do drugs. Some people are very open when it comes to sex, some drink alcohol. Where you see all these, there is witchcraft somewhere in the background. When a man is always getting drunk and cannot be delivered from alcohol, search for the witchcraft in his background determined to waste his soul. There was a lady whom we ministered to. The Lord said, **"there is prostitution in her root, and her mother (if she would be willing to tell her daughter the truth) used to prostitute herself"**. The lady was a highly promiscuous person who was always finding herself into sexual sins. When she looked into her background, she found out that her mother had not only prostituted, but was also deeply in witchcraft.

Every bewitched person is suffering from one type of addiction or the other, and it may not be alcohol, sex or drugs. A bewitched person may be addicted to an unholy relationship for example. Another person may be addicted to certain places, or certain items. The truth is - under every addiction is a hidden witchcraft.

There are some husbands who will never quit drinking and smoking until there is a revival in their own lives, because their wife is the one who satanically tied them to their addiction, just to ruin their lives. There are some men who will not be delivered

Addiction to manipulation; You may be under witchcraft influence if you are being manipulated, and unable to detect or break free from manipulation. For instance, a man knows his mother-in-law is manipulating their marriage, but is helpless, and in fact thinks the only way is to continue putting up with the manipulation. This is one of the ways witchcraft holds by manipulation.

Addiction to Flattery: This type of addiction is commonly found when men are under bewitchment. Satanic women will bring all sorts of high praises, to lock down the man. Most men who fall into the hands of witches are caught by the trap of flattery that they would sometimes prefer to hold onto flattery than to be set free from witchcraft.

Addiction to false churches: Many people attending satanic gatherings sometimes realize it. They talk about it.

They have memorized how the Lord spoke to them in several dreams, but they will not leave until all the virtues left in them are drained out.

Addictions come in many forms. The purpose of addiction is for the one addicted to be utterly destroyed by the substance/person whom they are addicted to.

PRAYERS

1. Every witchcraft addiction in my root be exposed, disgraced and be destroyed in the name of JESUS.
2. Foundational stronghold of addiction be broken in the name of JESUS
3. Every witchcraft substance that I have consumed, be exposed and be destroyed in the name of Jesus
4. Poison in my body, be flushed out by the blood of Jesus.
5. Witchcraft manipulation of my destiny through any form of addiction, catches fire in the name of Jesus.
6. Satanic ties are broken by the blood of Jesus.
7. My destiny, you are free from all sorts of addictions in the name of Jesus.
8. I am set free from all forms of manipulation in the name of Jesus.
9. I am delivered from the web of addiction in the name of Jesus.
10. Father, let your blood speak for me, deliver my soul completely from the chains of addictions in the name of Jesus.

NOTE

7

~

WITCHCRAFT &

DESOLATION

Witchcraft is the enemy of all things growth whether spiritual, financial, mental or emotional. Desolation and chronic poverty is sometimes a symptom of witchcraft activity. Many successful professionals have found whom they thought was "the love of their life" and after marriage, their successes vanish and poverty comes in. Anyone who has unresolved witchcraft in their foundation (a parent was living in witchcraft, or grandparent or somewhere in the ancestry) carries the spirit of desolation. Those currently living in active witchcraft carry the spirit of desolation too. There is no way a man marries or woman marries anyone in witchcraft and there will not be an entry into poverty.

Witchcraft is terrible and invites poverty into people's lives. For some families, everything is going well until they hire a maid or driver who is in witchcraft, everything goes down the drain. For some, their lives are flying high and until they become friends with a witch. For some, their destiny is in the right motion until they begin to attend a witchcraft infested church. For some, all is well until they change workplaces. For some, it all goes well until they move into a new neighborhood of witches and sorceries. Witchcraft works closely with the spirit of desolation.

When a witchcraft is in charge, there is utter desolation. The covenant of God's blessing does not abide where there is witchcraft. Until witchcraft is cast out will the covenant come to place. This is the reason why some families are deeply in poverty, because the husband or wife is in witchcraft, and witchcraft hates all things good.

Where there is hard work, diligence with finances, and there is rag, financial loss, business loss, economic disadvantage, there is witchcraft somewhere close. A man or woman of destiny will never be able to move forward into spiritual, mental, financial, emotional abundance where witchcraft is thriving.

ENEMY OF GROWTH: SPIRITUAL DESOLATION

Witchcraft hates growth. This is why some attend a church where they are expecting spiritual growth but they attain such. This is witchcraft. This is what happened to the Galatians. They had experienced spiritual growth, and they suddenly began to disobey. Paul recognized the root causes as bewitchment.

Galatians 3:1 NKJV

O foolish Galatians! Who has bewitched you that you should not obey the truth, before whose eyes Jesus Christ was clearly portrayed among you as crucified?

It is the same spirit of witchcraft that seeks to hinder Church growth. However, there is the promise of God that the gates of hell shall not prevail over the church. Hence, any Church facing such attacks needs to deal with witchcraft speedily.

ENEMY OF GROWTH: FINANCIAL DESOLATION

Witchcraft swallows finances, introduces debt, fuels impulsive spending, introduces sickness where the captive will spend and waste money until drained. Witchcraft is the enemy of excellence. It seeks to cut away excellence.

Nahum 2:2 NKJV

For the Lord will restore the excellence of Jacob
Like the excellence of Israel,
For the emptiers have emptied them out

And ruined their vine branches.

Wherever there is witchcraft activities, captives usually see symptoms such as the following:

1. The spirit of rag: Good things turn to rag easily. Some people have found out their properties soon become like rags despite their best effort to care for things.
2. Marital turbulence: Some husbands have witches as their girlfriends, and the witches outside begin to afflict the wives with illnesses.
3. Sicknesses: Sometimes witches continue to plant diseases such that captives never get healed. When they get healed, it is temporary.
4. Fight: Some witches have confessed to using satanic devices to send raging demons into the lives of couples such that couples who once had a peaceful home begin to fight and turn violence.
5. Disobedient children : Witchcraft specializing in turning the hearts of children away from the ways of obedience.

PRAYERS

1. Finger of God, deliver me from the pangs of desolation in the name of Jesus.
2. Finger of God, expose all witchcraft powers stealing by blessings.
3. Flaming fire of God, devour all powers stealing my blessings in the name of Jesus.
4. Witchcraft powers turning the sweetness of my life to bitterness, Father, project bitterness and immediate death into their lives
5. Witchcraft and counterfeit promotion, my life is not your portion in the name of Jesus.
6. Witchcraft agents of glory exchange, the finger of God retrieves my glory back from your hand in the name of Jesus.
7. Witchcraft powers turning my goodness into rags, are exposed and consumed by the fire of Yahweh in the name of Jesus.
8. Every unspoken affinity with poverty, be shattered in the name of Jesus.
9. Every unspoken affinity with lack, be shattered in the name of Jesus.
10. Father, reveal to me all witchcraft devices of poverty in my possession in the name of Jesus

11. Father, reveal unto me every loophole in my life that has been an entry point for witchcraft affliction in the name of Jesus.
12. Powers of the strongman holding on to my divine blessings, catch fire and I recover my goods back in the name of Jesus.
13. My finances will no longer be disabled in the name of Jesus.
14. Powers of rags, be destroyed in the name of Jesus.
15. Powers stealing essence from me, you are utterly ruined by the fire of the Holy Spirit in the name of Jesus.
16. Witchcraft powers swallowing my goodness, let the blazing sword of the Lord locate you for utter destruction in the name of Jesus.
17. I barricade these prayers with the blazing sword of the Lord in the name of Jesus.
18. By the ordinance of Yahweh, I prophesy and end all witchcraft activities in my life and family in the name of Jesus.
19. My life is hidden in the name of Jesus
20. The Lord is my shield and buckler in the name of Jesus
21. I am perfectly hidden under the shadow of the Most High.

NOTE

8

~

EXTINGUISHING

WITCHCRAFT

No one can successfully war against darkness except God wars on their behalf. If you want to win the war against witchcraft, then you have to be ready to live your life in the picture of Romans 12:1. When you live as such, God kindles His fire within you.

Romans 12:1 NKJV
I beseech you therefore, brethren, by the mercies of God, that you present your bodies a living sacrifice, holy, acceptable to God, which is your reasonable service

---

WHY EXTINGUISH WITCHCRAFT

1. Witchcraft seeks to bring desolation upon families, communities and nations
2. Witchcraft seeks to desecrate upon glories, seeks to turn beautiful destinies into rottenness
3. Witchcraft is the designer of shame and disgrace, and seeks to shame God's children
4. Witchcraft is the designer of failure, and seeks to design failure for everyone living in God's truth
5. Witchcraft seeks to frustrate all efforts that men and women of destiny make towards their purpose

Hence, men and women who seek to protect their destiny and live in God's purpose must fight witchcraft through the fire of the Holy Spirit burning within them.

WAY TO IGNITE GOD'S FIRE

1. Build a worship altar: Live your life as a form of worship to God.Worship God in words, songs and all you do.
2. Study God's word, and grow in the word of God
3. Go on a God-seeking mission. You will find God through a deeper study of His word and through worship.
4. Learn how to dialogue with God. This is what prayer is all about.
5. Learn how God speaks to you and listen to Him.
6. Do not exalt anyone, or anything above God - no compromise.
7. Obey the Lord at all times.
8. Build an altar unto the Lord.

9. Find a church where God is present. Do not go to a church where you are not growing spiritually.
10. Eliminate fear and worry from your walk with God.

PRAYERS

1. Thunder of God, strike down every evil diviner against my life in the name of Jesus
2. Witchcraft spirits, drawing me in with pity, be totally exposed and destroyed by the thunder of God in the name of Jesus
3. Thunder of God, Fire of God, strike and consume all the witchcraft powers seated upon the calling of my life.
4. I unseat all wicked powers by the thunder of God from my destiny in the name of Jesus.
5. Thunder of God, strike down all satanic designers seeking to pollute my destiny
6. My life, you will not be open to darkness in the name of Jesus.
7. East wind of the Lord, unveil every masquerading witchcraft power covering itself up with false humility in the name of Jesus
8. East wind of the Lord, unveil every masquerading witchcraft power assigned to turn my lot into desolation in the name of Jesus.
9. Thou witchcraft power firing the arrows of humiliation and ridicule, hear the word of God, Jesus Christ has made an open show off principalities and power, therefore let the hand of God my Father decorate you with the ultimate

height of humiliation and ridicule, in the name of Jesus.

10. My Father, deliver me by your righteous right hand from the grip of every witchcraft power in the name of Jesus.

11. My Father, deliver my destiny completely from the circles of witchcraft in the name of Jesus.

12. Thunder of God, strike and scatter the association of witchcraft assigned against me in the name of Jesus

13. Thunder of God, strike down all the gatherings of witchcraft sitting upon my glory in the name of Jesus

14. Thunder of God, strike all witchcraft agents assigned to my life in the name of Jesus.

15. Thunder and fire of God, strike and consume all witchcraft powers repelling goodness away from me in the name of Jesus.

16. My Father, regardless of how many ways witchcraft powers rise up against me, thou Man of War, consumes them 100 times more in the name of Jesus.

PRAYERS TO SPEEDILY EXTINGUISH WITCHCRAFT POWERS WORKING AGAINST YOUR MARRIAGE

Before starting prayers

These prayers are for those whom the enemy is tormenting in their marriage through witchcraft takeover. You must be legally married to your spouse. You cannot pray these prayers if you are not married.

Repent from all known sins.

Confess one by one as you remember them to God. The Lord will answer your prayers speedily will your prayers

Worship

Whenever you set up an altar of worship, the Lord comes down. Spend 12 minutes in worship before you say the prayers.

.

1. Father, let your fresh fire come upon my marriage in the name of Jesus
2. Father, let your fire power come upon my marriage in the name of Jesus
3. Father, let your
4. My Father, let your fire consume all other fire kindled against my marriage in the name of Jesus
5. Let the voice of the Lord, divide and consume satanic fire kindled in the heart of my spouse in the name of Jesus
6. Father, let your finger gather together all the devices of witchcraft used to bewitch my spouse and let the Lord consume them in the name of Jesus.
7. Satanic devices used to control my spouse (mention your spouse name), catch fire in the name of Jesus.
8. Fire of the Holy Spirit, come upon our household in the name of Jesus.
9. Finger of God, expose and devour the witchcraft agents of strife sent against my marriage in the name of Jesus
10. Let the flaming fire of God come upon all witchcraft agents sitting upon the joy of my marriage for destruction in the name of Jesus.
11. Flaming fire of God, burn to ashes all witchcraft powers sponsoring infidelity in my marriage in the name of Jesus.
12. Finger of God, unmask all masked witchcraft agents stealing from my marriage in the name of Jesus.
13. Finger of God, pull down witchcraft altars in my marriage in the name of Jesus.

14. Fire of God, burn up all concealed witchcraft hidden in plain sights in the name of Jesus.

15. Thou consuming fire, kindle your fire amongst the gathering of witches, planning against my marriage in the name of Jesus.

16. Father, overturn the cauldron of witchcraft in our community and our nation by the fire of the Holy Ghost in the name of Jesus.

17. Community witchcraft, be disgraced by the fire of the Holy Ghost.

18. Fire of revival, burst forth across this land, by the fire of the Holy Spirit in the name of Jesus.

BECOME A PART OF OUR DIGITAL COMMUNITY

Deliverance, Prophetic Ministry or Prophetic Worship Education

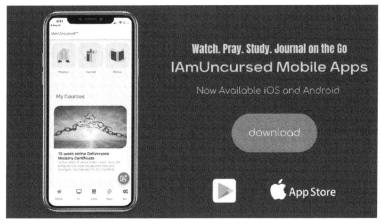

BECOME A PART OF OUR DIGITAL COMMUNITY

Deliverance and Family Altar Devotionals

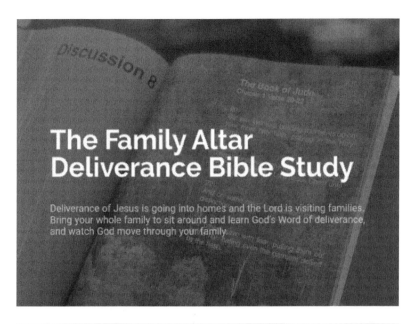

BECOME A PART OF OUR BUSINESS COMMUNITY

Business Courses

Startup Trainings, Financial Markets and Stock Trading Courses from the

EBENEZER GABRIELS LEADERSHIP EDUCATION

Unprofaned Purpose™

Innovation, Authority and Higher Leadership

Ascension into Purpose Begins Here

EXPLORE THE EBENEZER GABRIELS LEADERSHIP EDUCATION COURSES

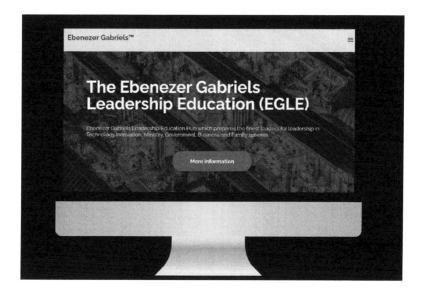

MARRIAGE EDUCATION
PRE-MARRIAGE EDUCATION COURSES
MARRIAGE DELIVERANCE COURSES
MARRIAGE READINESS PROGRAMS
www.blissfulmarriageuniversity.com
Download Blissful Marriage App

The Blissful Marriage App offers digital tools to convert all the lessons and knowledge you have received through this book into daily practice to transform your marital life.

Download the App for unlimited access unlimited marriage video library

Blissful Marriage Hosts Events – Conferences, Marriage Worship and Prayer Retreats, Marriage

Deliverance Programs, and other Marriage
Enrichment Program.

OTHER BOOKS BY

Ebenezer Gabriels and Abigail Ebenezer-Gabriels

Worship

Worship is Expensive

War of Altars

Business

Unprofaned Purpose

Building Business Altars

The Elements of Time

Marriage

Heaven's Compass to Building a Godly Premarital Atmosphere for Him

Heaven's Compass to Building a Godly Premarital Atmosphere for Her

Heaven's Gateway to a Blissful marriage for Him

Heaven's Gateway to a Blissful marriage for Her

Deliverance from the Yokes of Marital Ignorance

Pulling Down the Strongholds of Evil Participants in

Marriage

Heaven's Perspective on Blended Family

Prophetic

Activating Your Prophetic Senses

Dreams and Divine Interpretations

Family Deliverance

Uncursed

Deliverance from the Yoke of Accursed Names

Deliverance from the Curse of Vashti

Deliverance from the Yoke of Incest

Deliverance from the Wrong Family Tree

Mind

Deliverance from the Yokes Deep Mysteries of Creation in the Realms of Thoughts, Imaginations and Words

Spiritual War and Prayers

Rapid Fire

The Big Process called Yoke

Deliverance of the Snares of the Fowler

The only Fire that Extinguishes Witchcraft

No longer Fugitives of the Earth

Subduers of the Earth

Prayers of the Decade

Growth and Advancing in Faith

Deeper Mysteries of the Soul (English, Spanish, Arabic and Chinese)

Men: Called out of the Dunghill

Women: Bearers of Faith

New Beginnings in Christ

Wisdom my Companion

Deeper Mysteries of the Blood

Nations and intercessions

The Scroll and the Seal

America: The Past, the Present and the Next Chapter

Herod: The Church and Nigeria

Prophetic Insights into the Year

21 Weapons of Survival for 2021

2022 Meet the God Who Saves Blesses Shepherds and Carries

About the Authors

Ebenezer Gabriels is a Worshiper, Innovation Leader, Prophetic Intercessor, and a Computer Scientist who has brought heaven's solutions into Financial markets, Technology, Government with his computational gifts. Prophet Gabriels is anointed as a Prophetic Leader of nations with the mantle of healing, worship music, national deliverance, foundational deliverance, complex problem-solving and building Yahweh's worship altars.

Abigail Ebenezer-Gabriels is Pastor, Teacher, Worshiper and a Multi-disciplinary leader in Business, Technology, Education and Development. She is blessed with prophetic teaching abilities with the anointing to unveil the mysteries in the Word of God. She is a Multi-specialty Speaker, with a special anointing to explain Heaven's ordinances on earth.

Both Ebenezer Gabriels and Abigail Ebenezer-Gabriels are the founders of the Ebenezer Gabriels Schools of the Holy Spirit and are the Senior Pastors of LightHill Church Gaithersburg, Maryland.

They lead several worship communities including the 6-Hour Worship unto Deliverance, Innovation Lab Worship encounters, Move this Cloud - and prophetic podcast communities including the Daily Prophetic Insights and Prophetic Fire where God's agenda for each day is announced and the manifold wisdom of God is revealed on earth. Both Ebenezer Gabriels and his wife, Abigail Ebenezer-Gabriels joyfully serve the Lord through lifestyles of worship and their mandate is to build worship altars to intercede for nations.

Ebenezer-Gabriels Digital Communities

Explore the Ebenezer Gabriels Platforms

Spiritual War and Deliverance: *www.IAmUncursed.com*

Marriage: *www.Blissfulmarriageuniversity.com*

Children's: *www.inspiremylittleone.com*

Business and Marketplace: *www.unprofanedpurpose.com*

Ebenezer Gabriels Schools of the Holy Spirit and On Demand TV : *www.ebenezergabriels.org*

About Ebenezer Gabriels

At Ebenezer Gabriels Ministries (EGM), we fulfill the mandate of building worship altars by sharing the story of the most expensive worship ever offered by Jesus Christ, the Son of God and dispersing the aroma of the knowledge of Jesus Christ to the ends of the world.

Explore the Ebenezer Gabriels Communities

Deliverance: www.iAmuncursed.com
Singles: compass.blissfulmarriageuniversity.com
Marriage: www.Blissfulmarriageuniversity.com
Children's: www.inspiremylittleone.com
Business: www.unprofanedpurpose.com
Prophetic Evangelistic and Discipleship Missions: www.ebenezergabriels.org

Ebenezer Gabriels Publishing delivers biblically grounded learning experiences that prepare audiences for launch into their prophetic calling. We create educational contents and deliver in innovative ways through online classrooms, apps, audio, prints to enhance the experience of each audience as they are filled with the aroma of Christ knowledge and thrive in their worship journey.

EGM currently operates out of Gaithersburg in Maryland,

USA.

Made in the USA
Middletown, DE
06 October 2022

12104975R00073